DISCOVERING PLANTS AND FLOWERS

Storey Publishing

Are You Ready to Learn about
PLANTS?

Step outside and you'll find all sorts of plants waiting for you. From parks and meadows to woodlands and trails, to gardens and city streets, flowers and plants are everywhere. Grab this book and head out to start discovering!

THINGS TO BRING IN YOUR BACKPACK

This book and magnifying glass

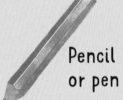

Pencil or pen

Camera

Local plant guide

Water bottle

Sunscreen or hat

Snacks

HOW TO HAVE FUN WITH THIS BOOK

Make a FLOWER CROWN

PAINT with plants

Learn how to WEAVE with plants

Go on a SCAVENGER HUNT

Use the MAGNIFYING GLASS for a closer look

Gather BERRIES to eat

Pick a FLOWER BOUQUET to cheer up a friend

Act like a BEE

PLANT PATCH STICKERS

There are 12 patch stickers in the back of this book that match **I SEE IT!** circles on some of the pages. When you see a type of plant or flower that matches something on an **I SEE IT!** page, put the sticker on the matching circle. See how many you can find!

Place the patch sticker on the circle!

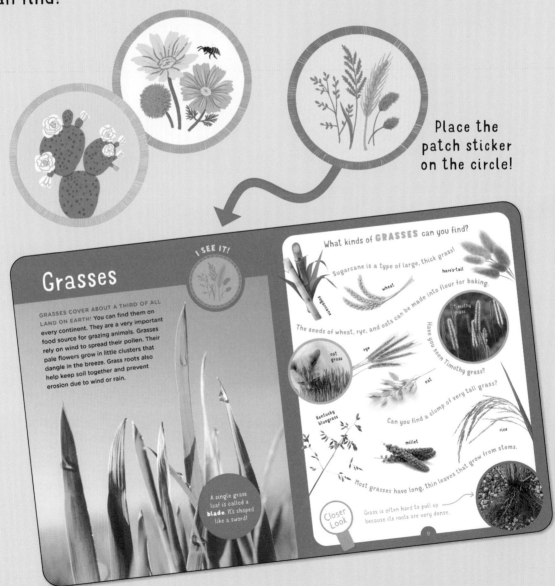

I SEE IT!

Grasses

GRASSES COVER ABOUT A THIRD OF ALL LAND ON EARTH! You can find them on every continent. They are a very important food source for grazing animals. Grasses rely on wind to spread their pollen. Their pale flowers grow in little clusters that dangle in the breeze. Grass roots also help keep soil together and prevent erosion due to wind or rain.

A single grass leaf is called a **blade.** It's shaped like a sword!

What kinds of **GRASSES** can you find?

Sugarcane is a type of large, thick grass!

sugarcane

wheat

hare's-tail

The seeds of wheat, rye, and oats can be made into flour for baking.

cat grass

rye

oat

Timothy grass

Have you seen Timothy grass?

Kentucky bluegrass

Can you find a clump of very tall grass?

millet

rice

Most grasses have long, thin leaves that grow from stems.

Closer Look

Grass is often hard to pull up because its roots are very dense.

9

Plants and Flowers
DISCOVERY TIPS

LOOK FOR FLOWERS OF
different sizes, shapes, and colors.

**SNIFF OUT DIFFERENT
FLOWER SCENTS.**
Which is your favorite?

NOTICE THE SHAPES
of all kinds of leaves.

LISTEN FOR BUZZING BEES
and watch how they
pollinate blossoms.

Don't pick
flowers without
permission.

BE CAREFUL
around thorny, prickly, and
poisonous plants.

Flowers

FLOWERS GROW IN SO MANY AMAZING COLORS AND SHAPES. Some flowering plants, like lupines and snapdragons, grow many blossoms on each stem. Others, like tulips and sunflowers, have just one head per stem. Blossoms may be shaped like stars, cups, bells, tubes, funnels, wheels, and more.

Another word for flower is **BLOSSOM**.

Have you seen any of these FLOWERS?

cherry blossoms

wild rose

poppy

Flowers can grow on trees or in the ground.

daisy

iris

delphinium

foxglove

Have you seen a blossom that looks like a bell?

borage

snapdragon

bleeding heart

trumpet vine

Do you have a favorite flower color?

Closer Look

The green sepals under a flower help keep the bud safe before it blooms.

PARTS OF A FLOWER

A plant has different parts that do different jobs so the plant can grow and stay healthy. Check out the parts of this iris.

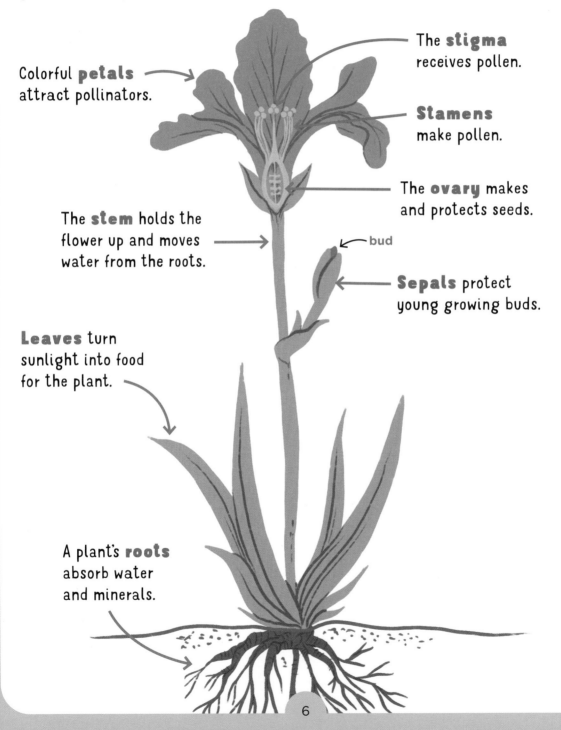

The **stigma** receives pollen.

Colorful **petals** attract pollinators.

Stamens make pollen.

The **ovary** makes and protects seeds.

The **stem** holds the flower up and moves water from the roots.

bud

Sepals protect young growing buds.

Leaves turn sunlight into food for the plant.

A plant's **roots** absorb water and minerals.

WATCH A FLOWER GROW

1 A sleeping **seed** lies on the ground. In the spring, rain and sunshine wake it up.

2 As **roots** push into the soil, a small **shoot** sprouts upward.

3 The roots grow longer. The shoot thickens into a **stem**. **Leaves** and flower **buds** form.

4 When the **flowers** bloom, insects come to pollinate them.

5 The flowers develop **seeds** that fall to the ground to make more flowers.

Grasses

GRASSES COVER ABOUT A THIRD OF ALL LAND ON EARTH! You can find them on every continent. They are a very important food source for grazing animals. Grasses rely on wind to spread their pollen. Their pale flowers grow in little clusters that dangle in the breeze. Grass roots also help keep soil together and prevent erosion due to wind or rain.

A single grass leaf is called a **blade**. It's shaped like a sword!

What kinds of **GRASSES** can you find?

Sugarcane is a type of large, thick grass!

sugarcane

wheat

hare's-tail

The seeds of wheat, rye, and oats can be made into flour for baking.

Timothy grass

cat grass

rye

Have you seen Timothy grass?

oat

Kentucky bluegrass

Can you find a clump of very tall grass?

millet

rice

Most grasses have long, thin leaves that grow from stems.

Closer Look

Grass is often hard to pull up because its roots are very dense.

NATURE WEAVING

Here's a fun way to make a beautiful weaving using grasses and plants. You'll need some yarn or string and a small branch shaped like a Y. Gather a handful of long grass stems and a bunch of flowers and leaves.

1 Tie one end of a long piece of yarn to the base of the branch. Wrap the yarn around the arms of the Y and tie the other end to the top of one of the arms.

2 Weave long stems of grass through the yarn, going over and under the lines.

3 Decorate the grass with blossoms, leaves, and other natural objects.

Leaves

FROM THE TREES ABOVE US TO THE GRASS BELOW, we are surrounded by leaves. Most of them are flat and green, but they have many different shapes and textures. Leaves may have smooth or toothy edges and be rounded or pointy. The job of a leaf is to turn the sun's energy into food the plant can use to grow.

The top of a tree is called its **crown**. The top layer of a forest is called the **canopy**.

What kinds of **LEAVES** can you find around you?

rose

hosta

maple

A simple leaf grows off the stem in a single shape.

dandelion

Pine needles are leaves!

pine needles

ivy

Compound leaves split off the stem into smaller leaflets.

palm frond

cedar

wood sorrel

spotted deadnettle

Have you seen a heart-shaped leaf?

Closer Look

Pick a green leaf and look for its thin veins. Some of those veins carry water up from the plant's roots. Others move sugar around.

WHAT DOES A PLANT EAT?

Plants make their own food using sunlight! This process is called photosynthesis.

SUNLIGHT

OXYGEN

CARBON DIOXIDE

FOOD

WATER

A plant's green leaves trap energy from the sun. They use that energy to turn **water** and **carbon dioxide** (a gas) from the air into **food**.

As they use the sun's energy, plants release another gas called **oxygen**. Humans and other animals breathe in oxygen and breathe out carbon dioxide, which plants use to make more food and oxygen. Everybody wins!

Photosynthesis means using light (*photo*) to put together something useful (*synthesis*).

How Does a
PLANT BREATHE?

See how a leaf gives off oxygen with this easy science experiment! All you need is a clear bowl or cup full of water, a freshly picked leaf, and a sunny spot.

1 Pluck a hand-size leaf from a tree or plant. Put it in the bowl of water right away, making sure most or all of the leaf is underwater. You may need to put a little rock on top to keep it submerged.

2 Place the bowl in a patch of sunlight. Now you have to be patient and wait a few hours.

3 Check your leaf! Do you see tiny bubbles all over the leaf's surface? Those bubbles are oxygen molecules leaving the plant.

Cactuses

MOST CACTUSES ARE DESERT PLANTS. They grow in dry places that get little rain, so they have special adaptations to help them store water. Cactuses come in all shapes and sizes. Their tough stems are extra thick from the water they keep inside. Most are covered in sharp spines to keep hungry animals away.

A cactus spine is a special type of hard, sharp leaf.

Have you seen any of these **SPIKY** plants?

Some birds nest in holes in big saguaros.

saguaro

Western screech-owl

cholla

organ pipe

Some cactuses attract pollinators like bats, birds, and insects.

ocotillo cactus flower

kingcup cactus flowers

fairy castle cactus

Dragonfruit grows on a cactus!

Have you seen a cactus plant growing indoors?

Closer Look

A cactus's thick ridges help catch rainwater and send it straight down to the plant's roots.

Wildflowers

A WILDFLOWER IS A PLANT THAT GROWS NATURALLY IN THE WILD, year after year. Unlike many garden flowers, wildflowers don't need human help to grow. Wildflowers are native to particular areas, but sometimes they may grow where they don't belong. A wildflower growing where a person doesn't want it to might be called a weed.

Wildflowers often grow in meadows.

How many kinds of **WILDFLOWERS** can you find while taking a walk?

aster

blanket flower

Wildflowers come in many colors.

chicory

goldenrod

Dandelion means "lion's teeth," which comes from its pointy leaves.

butterfly weed

dandelion

Monarch butterflies lay their eggs on milkweed plants.

milkweed

columbine

buttercup

trillium

Closer Look

Peer into a flower blossom. Can you find the sticky yellow pollen inside?

Make a FLOWER CROWN

Become a festive fairy or garden royalty!

1 Collect bunches of long, soft grasses and tall, flexible plant stems. Pick a few bright blossoms for decoration.

2 Take a handful of stems and line up the ends.

Tip: Tie the ends together with a short piece of string or yarn.

3 Holding the stem ends, start twisting. You might need to ask for help getting the twist started. Keep twisting until you have a circle.

4 If the crown fits your head, tie the ends together. If you need it to be longer, weave more stems into the loose ends of the bunch.

5 Decorate with flower "jewels" and fern or grass "feathers"!

Try making a slit in the stem of daisies or dandelions to chain them together.

Marsh & Water Plants

WHEN YOU VISIT A MARSH, POND, OR CREEK, you'll find all sorts of cool plants that grow on, under, or near water. Some wetland-loving plants, like cattails and rushes, are emergent, which means part of the plant pokes out of the water. Other plants, like fanwort, grow completely underwater. Some, like water lilies, float on the water's surface like little boats.

Water lilies

Water plants tend to grow fast because they get so much water and sunlight.

Have you discovered any of these WATER PLANTS?

marsh marigold

Guess what a skunk cabbage smells like? Skunk!

skunk cabbage

Have you ever seen a frog resting on a lily pad?

Water plants are food for many animals that live near water.

cattails

duck potato

water lily

Do you think cattails look like corndogs?

Closer Look

Twist a cattail's spike-shaped flower to release hundreds of tiny flying seeds!

BE A BOTANIST

A person who studies plants is called a botanist. One way botanists learn about plants is by sorting them into groups. If you aren't sure what a plant is, you can use the same clues that botanists do. You can use a field guide, or key, to help identify mystery plants if you know what to look for.

A simple leaf with smooth edges

A simple lobed leaf

A simple palmate leaf

Opposite leaves

Alternate leaves

Leaves with a whorl pattern

TOUCH IT

Reach out and gently pet different buds, leaves, stems, and petals. How do they feel against your hand? Check off each texture you find. (See pages 38–39 to learn about plants you shouldn't touch.)

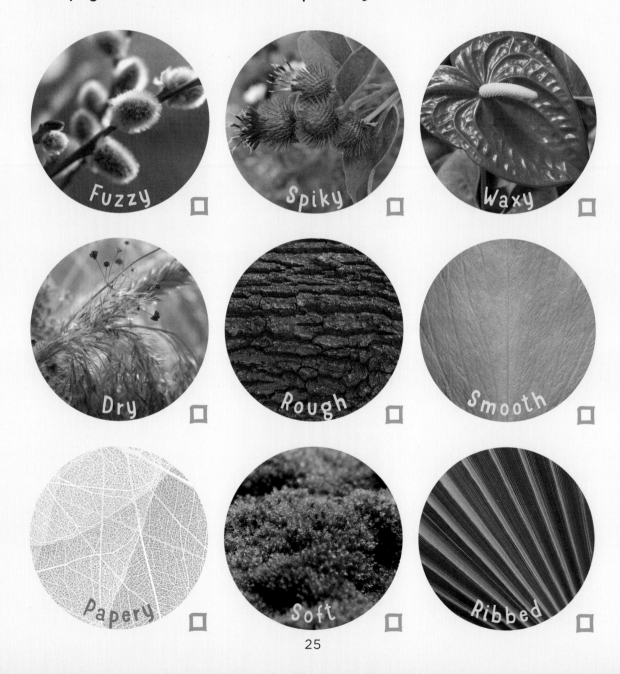

Fuzzy ☐

Spiky ☐

Waxy ☐

Dry ☐

Rough ☐

Smooth ☐

Papery ☐

Soft ☐

Ribbed ☐

Mosses & Ferns

I SEE IT!

MOSSES AND FERNS ARE ANCIENT PLANTS that were growing on Earth long before dinosaurs existed! They are different from most other plants because they do not make flowers or produce seeds. Instead, they make tiny spores that float away and grow into new plants. Moss plants grow super close together in thick mats, kind of like a carpet. Most ferns like to grow in shady forests.

A curled-up baby fern is called a fiddlehead because it looks like the end of a violin!

Look for **MOSSES** and **FERNS** in shady spots.

fiddleheads

sword fern

Can you find moss growing on a rock or tree trunk?

A fern leaf is called a frond.

bracken fern

club moss

common haircap moss

maidenhair fern

Gently touch some moss. How does it feel?

liverwort

Sphagnum moss can be used for bandaging wounds.

sphagnum moss

Closer Look

Check out the underside of a fern. Do you see any rows of teeny brown dots? They hold the plant's spores.

Making
PLANT ART

Leaves and flowers are like nature's crayons. Chlorophyll pigments make leaves green. Flowers come in all kinds of colors! When you rub soft leaves or flowers against a piece of paper, a little of that color comes off.

Here are some ideas for painting with plants. Before you begin, gather up some pieces of paper and crayons or markers.

BERRY GOOD

You've probably noticed how berries can turn your tongue purple or red when you eat them. Just imagine what you could paint with that juice. Sunsets! Dragons! Firework displays and flower bouquets! Get your creative juices flowing.

PAINT WITH PETALS

Gather flower petals of different colors and some grass or soft leaves. Crush the plants a little bit and press them on your paper like a paintbrush. Can you draw a flower or tree?

MAKE A DANDY LION

Pick a handful of dandelion flowers. Press down hard and rub the flowers on your paper until you have a big yellow circle. That's your lion's mane. Draw the eyes, ears, nose, and mouth. Now make your lion roar!

Berries

A BERRY IS A SMALL, JUICY FRUIT that is usually full of tiny seeds. Whether they are sweet or sour, wild berries are an important source of nutrition for many creatures. Birds, bears, rodents, and other animals cannot get enough of these delicious treats. Most people love berries, too!

As they ripen, berries change color from a pale greenish white to bright red, orange, purple, or blue.

What kinds of **BERRIES** have you tasted?

Have you ever gone berry picking?

mulberries

blackberry

blueberries

cranberries

Purple berries may stain your hands and tongue when you eat them.

serviceberries

These berries are all safe to eat, but some berries will give you a tummy ache.

wild strawberries

currants

What is your favorite berry?

gooseberries

wineberries

Closer Look

The hole in a raspberry shows where it was attached to the plant.

EAT PLANTS EVERY DAY!

Much of our food comes from plants. Some plants, like fruits and vegetables, you can eat raw. Others, like wheat, oats, and corn, may be ground into flour to make bread, pasta, and cereal. Cooking oils come from plants. So do sugar and maple syrup.

MAPLE SYRUP comes from trees.

The **JAM** for your toast is made of fruit.

Spaghetti is made from **WHEAT**.

TORTILLAS made from corn can be filled with beans and tomato salsa.

Sauce contains **HERBS** like basil and oregano.

STIR-FRIES are made with many different veggies.

RAINBOW COLOR SEARCH

See if you can spot a whole rainbow's worth of colors while looking at plants. Check off each one you find.

RED ☐

PINK ☐

ORANGE ☐

YELLOW ☐

GREEN ☐

BLUE ☐

PURPLE ☐

WHITE ☐

MAGENTA ☐

Pollinator Favorites

YOU HAVE PROBABLY SEEN BEES, BUTTERFLIES, AND OTHER INSECTS land on blooming flowers looking for sweet nectar to drink. Different flower types attract different pollinators. Bees love bright, fragrant flowers that grow in clusters. Moths go for pale night-blooming blossoms. Some bats and birds are also important pollinators.

Monarch butterfly

When insects spread pollen between blossoms, they help make seeds that grow into more flowers!

Have you seen these POLLINATORS visiting any flowers?

Many plants have sweet smells that attract flies and beetles.

ladybug

bottle fly

leaf beetle

bumblebee

blue tiger butterfly

Hummingbirds really like red flowers!

hummingbird

bee balm

rosy maple moth

Planting flowers will bring pollinators to your yard.

soldier beetle

black-eyed Susans

yarrow

coneflower

Closer Look

Can you see where a bee collects pollen on its legs?

POLLINATION STATION

Act like a bee (or butterfly) and help your favorite flowers grow! Go to a park or garden and find some blooming plants. Maybe there will already be pollinators around showing you what to do!

1 Peer into a blossom and find the dusty yellow or orange pollen on the flower's stamens.

2 Gently reach into the flower and rub your fingertip over the pollen.

3 Move to another flower of the same kind. Reach inside again, and this time gently rub your pollen-covered fingertip on the stigma. (It's the long skinny part in the middle.)

Hardworking bees visit hundreds of flowers each day! How many can you visit?

Butterflies collect pollen on their feet!

Don't bother the other pollinators. They won't sting you if you leave them alone to do their work.

Don't Touch!

LOTS OF ANIMALS EAT PLANTS, and because plants cannot run away from hungry mouths, some of them have ways to defend themselves. Some grow sharp spines or thorns to keep predators away. Others make poisonous sap or bitter fruit or leaves that are harmful to eat. Poison ivy and stinging nettle will give you a nasty rash if you touch them.

Have you ever had a thistle spine stuck in your finger?

Watch your step around these **DANGER PLANTS!**

A rose's thorns curve down to keep critters from climbing up the stem.

rose

Not sure what poison ivy looks like?

poison ivy

Remember the rhyme "Leaves of three, let me be."

poison oak

gorse

bramble

stinging nettle

Beware of a nettle's tiny stinging hairs!

Closer Look

Waxy holly leaves have tiny spikes that hurt to touch.

STRANGE PLANTS!

You probably won't find many of these unusual plants growing in your neighborhood, but such oddballs are definitely worth seeking out! You might find them in a botanical garden or greenhouse.

A REAL STINKER

Most flowers smell sweet and fresh, but not the **corpse flower**. Its 9-foot-tall blooms smell like rotten meat! Flies and beetles like the odor, though, and they come to pollinate the flowers.

This plant is taller than the tallest grown-up!

YUM, YUM!

Many animals eat plants, but did you know that some plants eat animals? **Pitcher plants** store a pool of watery fluid in a cup-shaped trap. When a bug falls in, it cannot escape and is slowly digested. **Venus flytraps** use snap traps to catch and eat their prey.

Venus flytrap

pitcher plant

FEELING SHY

If you touch a **sensitive plant**, you can watch its little leaves fold up and "play dead."

VERY OLD

Horsetails are among the oldest plants on Earth. They have been around for more than 300 million years.

A TRUE SURVIVOR

The **resurrection plant** shrivels into a dry little ball during periods of drought. It can go several years without water but opens up after a rainfall.

Edible Plants

YOU EAT PLANTS EVERY DAY. You know that a snack of carrot sticks or apple slices comes from plants. Did you know that popcorn, French fries, rice, peanut butter, and chocolate all come from plants? And the animals that provide us with meat and dairy products eat plants, too. We can't live without plants!

A healthy diet includes all the colors of the rainbow!

Which of these **PLANTS** have you **EATEN**?

green beans

broccoli

tomatoes

Plants that add flavor to food are called herbs.

basil

mint

parsley

chives

The parts of carrots and potatoes you eat are the plant's roots.

carrots

potato

What's your favorite vegetable?

Closer Look

The next time you eat a cucumber or sweet pepper, look for the seeds inside.

PARTS OF A SALAD

Ready for a snack? Try making a tasty salad
using various parts of plants.

Start with a base of **leaves**. You can use any type of lettuce, cabbage, kale, or spinach.

Add some **roots**! Shredded carrots and beets add color to the green.

For **fruit**, try some berries or grapes (or raisins, which are dried grapes). Tomatoes are fruits, too!

Get your **stems** in with some celery.

Top it off with some crunchy pumpkin or sunflower **seeds**!

SMELL IT

Start sniffing and let your nose lead the way through the wonderful world of plant smells. See if you can smell some of these scents. Check off each one you find.

Sweet ☐

Peppery ☐

Fruity ☐

Minty ☐

Flowery ☐

Grassy ☐

Woodsy ☐

Earthy ☐

Leafy ☐

Seeds

FLOWERING PLANTS MAKE SEEDS THAT GROW INTO NEW PLANTS. A seed's tough coat protects the sleeping baby plant, or embryo, inside until it is ready to grow. Seeds need sunlight, warmth, and water to "wake up" and start growing. When a seed senses those things, it sends a root down into the ground to suck up water and a shoot up out of the soil to gather sunlight.

Seeds can be spread by wind, water, and even animal poop!

How many types of **SEEDS** can you find?

sycamore tree seeds

dandelion seeds

Some seeds have wings or tiny parachutes that help them fly.

Burrs stick to animal fur and hitch a ride to new places to grow.

lotus seeds

pine cone

burrs

globe thistle seed

Have you ever eaten a poppy seed muffin?

poppy seeds

People and birds love to munch on sunflower seeds.

Closer Look

At the end of each thistle puff is a teeny-tiny seed waiting for the wind to blow it somewhere new.

BRIGHTEN SOMEONE'S DAY!

Let someone special know you're thinking of them by picking a small bouquet of flowers.

Look for wildflowers on a walk or visit your garden if you have one. You can gather a mix of colors or pick all of one kind. A handful of dandelions or violets can bring love and cheer!

MY LIST OF PLANTS

Make a list of some of the plants and flowers you find.

Plant name: _____ Date/Time: _____

Where I saw it: _____

What I noticed about it: _____

Plant name: _____ Date/Time: _____

Where I saw it: _____

What I noticed about it: _____

Plant name: _____ Date/Time: _____

Where I saw it: _____

What I noticed about it: _____

Plant name: _____ Date/Time: _____

Where I saw it: _____

What I noticed about it: _____

Plant name: _____ Date/Time: _____

Where I saw it: _____

What I noticed about it: _____

Plant name: _____ Date/Time: _____

Where I saw it: _____

What I noticed about it: _____

My favorite flower

Draw a picture of the flower you liked best on your plant walk.

Draw a pollinator that visited your flower.

MY DAY OF DISCOVERING PLANTS

Match up the stickers to what you did or found on your plant walk.

Made a plant weaving

Picked wild berries

Wore a flower crown

Saw a cactus

Found a fern

Made plant art

MY DAY OF DISCOVERING PLANTS

Match up the stickers to what you did or found on your plant walk.

Saw different shapes of flowers

Helped pollinators

Sorted leaves like a botanist

bleeding heart

alternate leaf pattern

sunflower

palmate leaf

honeybee

bracken fern

cactus

ladybug

flower crown

lobed leaf

wild rose

smooth-edged leaf

opposite leaf pattern

bluebell

berries

plant weaving

bee

coneflower

seeds

whorl leaf pattern

painting with flowers

monarch butterfly

milkweed

daffodil

geranium

blueberries

coneflower

sunflower

chive flower

elderberries

poppy

raspberry

sprout

anemone

blueberry bush

chicory

cattail

seeds

wheat

rabbit

honeybee

forget-me-not

wild strawberries

sweet pea

aster

fern spores

dandelion

nasturtium

blackberries

PLANT PATCH STICKERS

Look for these different plants. When you spot one, place your sticker on the matching circle where it says "I SEE IT!"

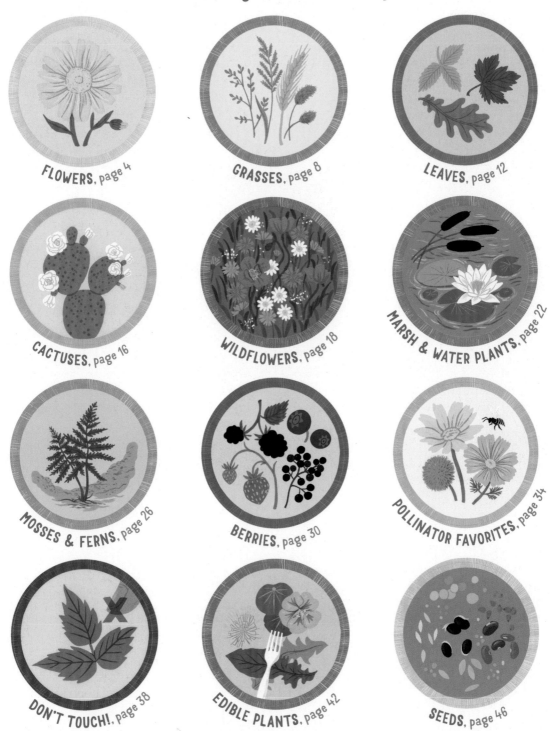

FLOWERS, page 4

GRASSES, page 8

LEAVES, page 12

CACTUSES, page 16

WILDFLOWERS, page 18

MARSH & WATER PLANTS, page 22

MOSSES & FERNS, page 26

BERRIES, page 30

POLLINATOR FAVORITES, page 34

DON'T TOUCH!, page 38

EDIBLE PLANTS, page 42

SEEDS, page 46

The mission of Storey Publishing is to serve our customers by
publishing practical information that encourages
personal independence in harmony with the environment.

Text by Kathleen Yale
Edited by Deanna F. Cook and Lisa H. Hiley
Art direction and book design by Erin Dawson
Text production by Jennifer Jepson Smith

Storey Publishing
210 MASS MoCA Way
North Adams, MA 01247
storey.com

Storey Publishing is an imprint of
Workman Publishing, a division
of Hachette Book Group, Inc.,
1290 Avenue of the Americas,
New York, NY 10104

Distributed in Europe by Hachette
Livre, 58 rue Jean Bleuzen, 92
178 Vanves Cedex, France

Distributed in the United Kingdom
by Hachette Book Group, UK,
Carmelite House, 50 Victoria
Embankment, London EC4Y 0DZ

ISBN: 978-1-63586-675-9
(paper over board with 3
sticker sheets, magnifying
glass, and fold-out journal)

Printed in Dongguan, China
by R. R. Donnelley on paper
from responsible sources
10 9 8 7 6 5 4 3 2

APS (10/24)

Library of Congress Cataloging-
in-Publication Data on file